Healing a Woman's Heart

8 Steps from Your Past to Your Purpose

Patricia K. Layton

Hannah, you
I pray this one day
read this one day
Very soon.
You ARE LOVED,
ALLOW GOD
TO HEAL
YOU ♡

2/28/19

Oh my goodness, Lord.
Your majesty overwhelms me.
Your mercy literally allows my life to go on.
Your grace covers my utter failure.
Your blessings astound me.
Your glory draws my arms to the sky.
Your use of my life brings my knees to the ground.
Your Word gives me direction.
Your power gives me freedom.
Your anointing makes me dance.
Your vision takes my breath away.
Your blood and Your sacrifice draw me to repentance.
Your death gives me life and Your life gives me purpose.
Your reflection challenges my pursuit of holiness.
Your supernatural power gives me rest.
Most of all, my Lord, Your love gives me all that I need.

Your Grateful Daughter, Pat

Also by Pat Layton:
Life Unstuck
Surrendering the Secret
A Surrendered Life

Events and Resources:
Imagine Me Set Free
Rest Quest
Freedom Quest

Patlayton.net

Note: Healing a Woman's Heart is a biblically based, eight-step healing journey that has been proven and praised by thousands of men and women worldwide. However, it cannot take the place of professional Christian counseling and pastoral leadership. If at all possible, it is best to work through this study with a friend, pastor, or small group. Healing happens best in community where you can be heard, cared for, and prayed for.

This product is also available in an ONLINE COURSE

Imagine Me...Set Free is available on author's website
SHOP https://patlayton.net

The content is the same but the course is in a Printable PDF Workbook Format.

> So teach us to number our days,
>   that we may gain a heart of wisdom.
> > > Psalm 90:12, NKJV

> I run in the path of your commands
>   for you have set my heart free!
> > > Psalm 119:32

> "But as for you, you meant evil against me; but God meant it for good, in order to bring it about as it is this day, to save many people alive."
> > > Genesis 50:20, NKJV

> "And you shall know the truth, and the truth shall make you free."
> > > John 8:32, NKJ

Contents

INTRODUCTION

I have been waiting, praying, and preparing because the Lord told me you were coming. He told me that you are a woman passionate for Him, a woman who wants to share the healing journey that He has taken you on with other women who are lost in their sin, lost in their pain, and lost in their past.

Some memories blazed on our hearts take only the slightest mention to roll warm, sweet joy into our minds. I have lots of those—the first time I ever saw my husband, the smell and softness of the first time I kissed each of my children, the day I placed my life on the altar to accept my saving faith, the sweet summer day that I surrendered the secret of my past.

Yes, dear sister, I know you, and I am honored to take this journey with you. I cannot wait to get your e-mail, see you at a conference, or talk with you on the phone. It will be like old times. I knew you would be here.

In my books, *Surrendering the Secret* and *Life Unstuck: Finding Peace with Your Past, Purpose in your Present, and Passion for your Future*, I devote entire chapters to help you, my friend, understand the critical step of letting God open the "casket of your heart" to heal and restore *anything* the enemy has captured from your life that hinders your *life unstuck,* your *freedom* in any way.

My desire for this book is another opportunity to share this life-saving biblical process, to take you by the hand and walk through each of the eight steps to healing and wholeness once and for all. We want this completely behind us. We want to be *free* to share the word of our testimony anytime, anywhere, with anybody! Right? Can you just imagine?!

I can. I have experienced firsthand the *freedom* that comes from having nothing to hide. Because of these eight steps, I enjoy having nothing to fear being uncovered, revealed, or worse yet, passed on to those I love.

You can too. I promise, using God's unmatched Word and His uncompromising desire to set you free, you will see *free*! You will know the dance-stirring joy of looking your past heartbreak right smack in the eye and saying, "Get thee behind me!"

So come on, friend, reach out and take hold of my hand through this journey; take the first step, then the next . . . until eight steps later . . . we dance!

Pat

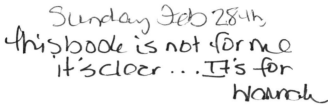

Sunday Feb 28th,
this book is not for me
it's closer ... It's for
Hannah

Step One: Say Yes!

It was a fabulous Florida day. Springtime. My windows were rolled down, and my Christian music was blaring. I was singing and praising God because I'd recently experienced a dramatic spiritual awakening. Within six months of my rebirth, my husband and two sons had also turned to Christ. Our lives had dramatically changed as a result, and it seemed that God was suddenly pouring out His blessings on our home and family. Things seemed to finally be taking a turn for the better after a long season of looming dead ends and pending divorce.

Little did I know that "secrets" of my past, long stuffed away, were about to all come crashing in and put my family at risk all over again.

My new Christian journey seemed to be affecting every part of my life, one of which was the radio station that broke into the air from my car speakers. I had moved from rock to praise music and was intrigued by the style of chatter between the radio moderators. They prayed. They quoted Bible verses. They teased about bad habits. I had jumped out of my car for a few minutes to run an errand. When I slid back into the driver's seat, my praise music had changed over to a talk show. I was shocked to hear three women talking with a moderator, sharing transparent stories about their past heartbreaks.

I could barely breathe as I listened. My heart raced. What

in the world was this? Why were they talking about their deepest secrets on a Christian radio station?

What does God have to do with this kind of ugliness?

What does this shameful pain have to do with God?

What had happened to my praise music?

Little did I know as I pulled my car to the side of the road to listen that my life would never be the same.

A few months later, after I'd successfully stuffed my emotions down again, I strolled in to the Christian bookstore with one thing in mind: to find a book that would help me fix my husband! He really needed fixing. We had been Christians for at least a year, and I just knew God still wanted to do a lot of work on him. As I stepped into the bookstore, I ran smack into a display of books all focused on one topic—you guessed it—MY SECRET. In a Christian bookstore. How could that be? I had made it through eight years and never seen that word, much less said it. At the time, I had no idea *why*, but I grabbed up the book, dashed to the register, paid the bill, and raced for the door.

Over the next five or six hours, I devoured that book from cover to cover. Although I can remember it like it was yesterday, it is close to impossible for me to describe the feelings that stirred around in my heart and mind over that day of reading. Shock, unbelief, fear, disgust, and certainly nausea are just a few that come to mind. After finishing, I fumbled my way to the bathtub and filled it halfway with scalding water. The rest of the tub, I filled with my own hot tears as I sobbed for hours. I wept for my loss. I wept for the lies. I wept for the author of the book I'd read. I wept for everyone involved. I wept for the world. I wept for the pain of my Savior, my Lord, and my

Redeemer, Jesus Christ.

When I had cried all that I could cry, I handed my heart to God.

You may be someone who can identify with those hours in my life. That process in time that I allowed God to shine His light into the darkest places of my past. I allowed Him, like He describes in Psalm 139, to "make even my darkness light to Him."

Maybe you, like me, experienced the devastation of a past personal choice. Maybe you have suffered abuse or abandonment in your past. Maybe it is childhood brokenness in your family. Rape. Substance abuse. Immorality. Adultery or divorce may have rocked your world so hard that you are still on shaky ground.

Wherever you fall in these descriptions, whatever has caused you to pick up this book or sign up for one of my courses, I pray that you will walk with me. Walk with me on a journey through healing and restoration. A journey of hope and a journey toward the full and final peace with your past that God has in mind for you.

It matters that you do. It matters to those who will hear the word of your testimony. It matters to your church, your community, and your calling. It matters to the world that you are *free*! That your past is behind you and now merely a tool in the hands of God to help someone else.

The Bible says in 2 Corinthians 1:4 that God actually *comforts* us in all of our troubles *so that* we can comfort those who are in trouble. God wants us to be set free from the bondage of our past, so our stories and our newfound freedom can be shared with others.

Let's get started by going backward.

Keeping the Past Where It Belongs

Strolling down memory lane can be wonderful. Memories come and go when we least expect them. The smell of warm baked bread takes us back to Grandma's house, and we're eight years old again. Attending a hometown high school reunion inspires us to drive up and down streets pointing out our elementary school, a dear friend's home, or our favorite burger hangout to a bored spouse or friend.

In the same way, bad memories—despite our efforts to suppress them—ebb and flow in our minds and hearts, bringing pain instead of happiness.

As I have implied, my most haunting memory concerns something I chose myself, not one inflicted upon me. My heartbreak was caused by an abortion I had when I was twenty-three years old. I remember the smell of the room, the looks on the faces of women sitting around a dark reception room, the sounds of soft lonely tears, and the coldness of the building. Oddly enough, I still remember the dirty tennis shoes worn by the "nurse" who shoved a clipboard with an intake questionnaire coldly in my direction, and my petrified flight out the door in search of a "nicer abortion." Unlike the sweet memories of elementary school, those darker memories have been seared deeply in my heart and soul for many years.

Tragically, traumatic memories have more than a passing impact on our lives. Research confirms my own experience. My own memories not only haunted me but caused daily damage in my life for years. The past holds some of us captive for decades.

After years of trying everything else to put the past behind me, I learned that *to experience healing, I had to go back and face my past*. Only then did I become free to move into the future. The thought of going back to deal with emotions I had worked so hard to bury frightened me and seemed overwhelming. What good could come from that? Why would anyone go back?

The Bible contains a story about a woman named Hagar. Hagar was a woman much like me and maybe like you. Her dream for family and motherhood did not go the way she planned—the way she had dreamed since she was a little girl.

A wife named Sarai owned Hagar, an Egyptian slave. Sarai could not have a child, so she persuaded her husband, Abram, to father a child through the slave girl. After Hagar became pregnant, she began to feel and act superior to her owner. "Then Sarai said to Abram, 'You are responsible for my suffering! I put my slave in your arms, and ever since she saw that she was pregnant, she has looked down on me. May the LORD judge between me and you.' Abram replied to Sarai, 'Here, your slave is in your hands; do whatever you want with her.' Then Sarai mistreated her so much that she ran away from her" (Genesis 16:5–6, HCSB).

We see that Hagar responded to what she saw as a hopeless situation by running away as hard and fast as she could. I don't think she stopped to consider where she might end up or what consequences her choice would bring. She just responded to her pain and loss—to the heartbreak that had been done *to her* by someone else—in desperation and panic. I can identify because I too have been Hagar.

Perhaps, like me, like thousands of women every day, you too have responded to your own heartbreak with panic. Perhaps you have run hard and fast from some poor moral choices, a bad marriage, a dead-end relationship, a messed-up ministry, or a crashing career. It may have been a choice that seemed to be your only hope, your only option, but desperation doesn't make for sound choices. Just like Hagar, many of us felt lost, alone. and betrayed. We ran, and with little direction, made a choice we will forever revisit.

We choose to run and hide for many reasons: as a response to shame about our behavior, our horrible circumstances, and lifestyle patterns; as an act of rebellion or control; or because we have been dealt an unfair hand by a husband, boyfriend, or parents. Maybe we choose escape to protect someone else or as an act of confused freedom. Many of us have been told that running away and keeping secrets is a simple solution to the problems of our heart.

Eventually we find out the truth. Secrets and hiding our heartaches lead us to the same place Hagar's choice to run led her, to the middle of nowhere.

My Story

My story wasn't so different. I had lived a life of bad choices and immorality since I was fifteen. I grew up in an average home with a mother and a father who were married as young twenty-somethings in rural Savannah, Georgia. My parents stayed married for over fifty years. Both have moved to heaven now but were middle-class, blue-collar, God-fearing folks. I have three younger sisters and lots of memories, both good and bad.

My parents also came from fairly average American families—neatly woven on the outside but fairly messed up underneath. Their family backgrounds included alcoholism, tobacco and drug addiction, pornography, divorce, adultery, and teen pregnancy, all of which affected their lives and mine. Maybe you can relate?

I've learned that family "junk" goes back to Adam and Eve and is truly God's specialty. He uses our personal junk to bring us to good and healed places. My teenage immorality led to a teenage marriage, teenage motherhood, eventual abandonment, and finally to becoming a single teenage mother of one simply precious son.

As I cared for my son, and with the help of my parents returned to school and college, I met the next "man of my dreams." The two of us continued in the lifestyle we had both grown accustomed to in the seventies and soon found ourselves in an unplanned pregnancy. The good news was that we were in love and engaged to be married when we found ourselves pregnant. The bad news was that even though I was in love and had agreed to be married, I was not in trust. I had already been left all alone holding a swaddling babe wrapped in a blanket. I was not about to go that route again.

I had fought diligently for "a woman's right to choose" while in college. During those days, I could wax eloquent about why women should have a right to determine when, and if, they wanted to have a child. I proclaimed we ultimately should control "our own bodies." I was so convincing that my opinions had even been published in a local woman's newspaper.

When I discovered I was pregnant just prior to my wedding day, I made what I thought was a logical and healthy decision, to abort. As far as I was concerned, my husband-to-be had no vote. He silently obliged, a choice we would both live to regret.

I told you earlier about my first visit to a newly opened neighborhood clinic that I deemed dirty and dark. That facility left such a nasty taste in my mouth, I decided to approach my own ob-gyn, the one who had delivered my firstborn son, to obtain the "safe and legal" abortion I had fought so hard to legalize.

Just like my future husband, my ob-gyn never questioned my decision. He simply set the date for two weeks after my wedding day. A marriage certificate meant little to me in terms of a man staying for the long haul, so I accepted the date. My husband and I went on our honeymoon pregnant, with a life changing date on our calendars when we returned. It was not the honeymoon of every little girl's dreams. The marriage would not be either, not for a very long time.

We planned to drop our son off at kindergarten and arrive at the hospital at 7 a.m. (My husband had begun the steps to adopt my son before we ever married.) I paid the extra money to be put to sleep during the procedure. Even with that, we were told the whole thing would only take "a few minutes". We planned to pick up our son at school, go get some lunch, and move on with life.

It would be our secret.

Instead, I woke up unable to move my body or speak. I had a tube stuck down my throat and a machine breathing for me. While my husband and my parents stood at the foot of my hospital bed, the doctor explained that I had an allergic reaction to the anesthesia. My breathing had stopped during surgery. I had to be admitted to the hospital. My new husband was forced to call my parents to pick up my son from school.

I still remember today the look on the faces of my mom and dad as they stood at the foot of my hospital bed. Shock. Shame. Fear. Loss. My secret was a secret no longer.

My feelings of embarrassment, shame, and even anger followed me out of that hospital. They did not leave for seven long years.

My parents never said the word *abortion*. I never said the word. My husband never said the word.

Perhaps there is a *word*, a choice, a violation, a heartbreak that you cannot bring yourself to say out loud. To do so would give it life, some sort of an invitation to enter your heart and life. I understand. I have been there.

What happened next would close the casket of my heart and change my life forever.

I'm guessing that no matter the nature of your *secret*, you know the term *"casket of your heart"* is more than just a mental picture. Depending on how long ago your heartbreak happened, you have probably kept your secret buried deep inside your heart. Even if someone knows your story, you most likely have never talked about it out loud. You have never wrestled verbally with the who, what, when, where, or why of your broken heart.

In this book I want to allow you the opportunity, or maybe the challenge, of digging into your memories for the purpose of discovering some new things about God.

Hagar learned in her situation. She trusted God and braved a return to her past. In the process, Hagar discovered a new identity for God and relationship to God.

I didn't know that choosing to run from my problems wasn't solving my problem. I was, rather, creating a whole new set of difficulties. Once we begin down the road of running, we have to run again and again. Like a modern-day Hagar, we run into the wilderness of fear, shame, abandonment, anger, and self-destruction. In a desolate, lonely land, we become numb captives to our secret. Even if it is a secret that somebody else caused.

Hagar's flight to the desert left her at a spring beside the road. The angel of the Lord met her there and told her to return to Sarai and submit to her authority.

"The angel also said, 'You are now pregnant and will give birth to a son. You are to name him Ishmael (which means 'God hears'), for the LORD has heard your cry of distress. . . .' Thereafter, Hagar used another name to refer to the LORD, who had spoken to her. She said, 'You are the God who sees me.' . . . So Hagar gave Abram a son, and Abram named him Ishmael" (Genesis 16:10–15, NLT).

Lessons from the Wilderness

As we compare the experience of Hagar to the wilderness we wander today, we realize that our secrets and the heartbreaks of our past do not lead to a literal desert. Instead, they create a wilderness we carry in our hearts and minds. When we carry a heavy burden, we naturally feel trapped by the shadows that surround us. *Like Hagar, we grow weary, and feel ready to give up in despair and shame.* As if that weren't enough, both Hagar's story and ours have a villain who always follows us into the wilderness. Instead of seeing the "God who sees me" and the only One who never lets us go, we hear the inner voices of condemnation and shame . . . and the lying voice of the tempter.

The amazing news is that God longs to come and rescue us. When God found Hagar abandoned and hopeless in the wilderness, He showed her that she must confront her pain and stop trying to mask it. For every woman, the mask looks a little different. God wants us to remove our masks, the pain we hide behind, and be *free*. He sets us free to love, free to heal, free to forgive, and free to live.

Some women feel the sting of their choices, and the choices made upon them, every day. Others have completely disconnected from them. No matter how silent your pain, God hears the cry of your heart. He sees you in your desert and feels your pain. God longs for you to look back on that difficult time in your life, and with Hagar to ask, "Have I truly seen the One who sees me?"

If you are a fellow traveler on the journey of recovery from a past of heartbreak and shame, I hope you will allow God to use me in your life. Through the next few pages of this book and the supporting online course, I will seek to be your guide, your angel in the desert, safely walking with you back to face the secrets, shadows, and shame that have kept you from the life God intended for you. Just like Hagar, you have a promise that God will personally meet you in your place of need.

The Bottom Line: Trusting the God Who Sees Me

Going back to find peace *isn't* easy. That is exactly why we resist. We continue to hesitate for many reasons. We doubt God's heart toward us. After all the pain and struggles in our lives we ask ourselves, *God is good, how could He have let this happen to me?* Given the way most of us were raised, we also focus on God's judgment with little understanding of His incredible desire and passion for us.

God longs to love you, and your love is safe with Him. His love is like nothing we have ever experienced. His love is unconditional and eternal. You can rest in God's arms, take comfort in His unfailing love, and hold His hand on your journey toward freedom.

Right now, make the choice for freedom. Say yes! Summon the courage and make a new choice, a choice for your freedom. Say yes! Choose the path of healing and peace; don't allow your life and dreams to die with a past mistake. Say yes!

Remember you are not alone. Think of reading this book, joining this online course, as a challenging mountain trek. Now is the time to confront the fear and pain and begin the slow, steady journey to the summit. It takes faith and courage to tackle this mountain. We're going to do this because the view from the top is worth the surrender.

These steps will help you to get to the summit where the stigma of your past is gone. In the process you will find personal healing or healing for someone you love. Together we can enjoy reconciliation with God and with others. In the process we find a life of secrets, shame, and shadows completely redeemed.

In step two, we'll take the first action by looking honestly at your personal story and how the past may be affecting your life. We'll dig into some things that may have been buried for a while. Some things may "stink" a little until the *light* has a chance to shine on them and reveal truth and healing.

Every woman who has chosen lies and wearing masks as a way of escape has been sold a lie. Lies create secrecy, bondage, darkness, and shame. God wants to set you free, but you will have to pursue your freedom through a sometimes-uncomfortable journey. You will not be alone. You have an entire team behind the pages of this book.

Action Step One: Looking Back

Take some time to consider some of the following questions that will stir your memories and your heart enough to begin the journey. This effort will certainly require trusting God to hold you tight and show you His purpose for leading you to this study.

Think a bit about how you keep "memories" of your past. Do you organize them in notebooks marked with the date and location of events, or are you more likely to drop them into randomly marked boxes? How about those of us who keep *thousands* of photos on our computers, photos we can only enjoy by scrolling through our desktop! Consider how you store physical memories.

This study is about memories of the heart. Are there some things that are rolling up in your head and heart as we talk about "going back"? Do you still have that "flight" response? Explain to those you are doing this study with or journal your feeling here:

Has your heart ever felt "closed like a casket" as I described in my story? When? Where?

Reread Genesis 16:1–15 from your own Bible.

How do you feel about the story of Hagar we discussed? How must Hagar have felt about her circumstances, herself, and those she should have been able to trust?

Have you *seen* the God who *sees* you? Can you point to a specific day or time when you "surrendered" your life to Christ and purposefully placed your life in God's hands?

Look up and write out these verses for extra support and join me on my website at www.patlayton.net for additional resources.

John 3:17, 21

Ezekiel 34:12, 1516

Luke 15:47

Step Two: Where Have You Come From?

The first time I remember getting caught in a lie I was about eight years old. We were at a cookout on the beach when all of a sudden, my sister started crying. (Insert the mental image of my most innocent look here.) I had *no* idea what happened. At least that was the report I gave my mother.

Little did I know that my mother had actually watched me drop a Fiddler crab into my sister's swimsuit. The crab had mostly scared my sister, but she acted like I was an ax murderer. I got into some major deep water with my mom for lying. Paradoxically, however, I was the one who was permanently scarred. Lies hurt others, but like a slow-dripping sip of acid, they eat us alive from the inside out.

No one has to teach a child to lie. In our fallen world, deception is the norm rather than the exception. We've practiced deception since Eve in the garden. People give many excuses. Some people lie for their own selfish gain, but I think most of the time, we lie out of fear in attempts to avoid exposure, loneliness, or vulnerability.

Children learn quickly that lying can get them into trouble. They either choose to be more truthful or resort to more lies, sneaking around or clamming up in silence. As adults, we continue in these same patterns. We all have secrets—things we've done we hope no one will ever know about. In the words of Paul the apostle, "Everyone has sinned; we all fall short of God's glorious standard" (Romans 3:23, NLT).

Every one of us hides something we don't want others to know about—something we're ashamed for them to know. The villain in our life story, the devil, knows that as long as he can keep us bound by our silence and secrets, he can keep us from the freedom God offers. As long as Satan can keep us isolated and separated from others, we automatically remain in bondage. A slogan in recovery programs says it well: We're as sick as our secrets.

As we learn to live in silence and secrecy, many of us end up with a stockpile of hurts that we've buried deep inside ourselves. The only way to overcome and to live free of those hurts is to learn to recognize the lies we've accepted as truth. As we root out each lie, we begin to replace them with the truth.

When Jesus said the truth would set us free (John 8:32), He expressed a double meaning. In the ultimate sense, we only find freedom in the person of Christ, who is the Truth. In a smaller sense, we find freedom bit by bit as we drain lies of their power and expose them to the truth.

Satan uses lies about God, our self-worth, other people, and the world to keep us limping with old infected wounds and trapped in unhealthy ways of living. Culture bombards us with myths and deceptions about sex, love, and life. That's why Jesus spoke strongly about the deceiver who plants so many lies in our world. Jesus said of the devil, "He was a murderer from the beginning and has not stood in the truth, because there is no truth in him. When he tells a lie, he speaks from his own nature, because he is a liar and the father of liars" (John 8:44).

The apostle Peter knew great failure and shame. After claiming special commitment and loyalty to Jesus, the brash apostle denied Him only hours later. Peter learned the hard way what he later wrote of the devil, "Be sober! Be on the alert! Your adversary the devil is prowling around like a roaring lion, looking for anyone he can devour" (1 Peter 5:8, HCSB).

The devil seeks to isolate and slowly destroy you. He is the master deceiver. With the benefit of millennia spent watching human nature, Satan takes advantage of our tendency to try to escape. He knows we will usually run away like Hagar did, rather than making the bold choice to confront our pain.

Unwilling to face our intense emotions or to take responsibility for our actions, we let our burdens become our identities. We accept lies about ourselves and about God. In the process, we settle for survival in place of real life. Keeping the secret allows the pain to slowly eat away at us. As a result, we often seek to self-medicate to provide some relief from the pain. Other times, we experience the opposite. Because we feel nothing, we use self-destructive behaviors just to feel something.

What about you? What means have you used to escape the pain or to feel through the numbness? Common options include: literally medicating with drugs (the most common of which is alcohol); behaviorally medicating through self-destructive actions; and in our darkest moments, attempts at suicide.

When tempted by these ploys and behaviors, we desperately need to remember who our enemy is. Satan strategically uses the wounds in our lives. He strives to distort our identities. He knows our vulnerabilities and takes advantage of our weaknesses. If Satan can keep us feeling worthless, keep us feeling guilty, or keep our minds and hearts under his influence, he can keep us from the glory God intended.

Satan seeks to separate us from the intimacy God wants us to share. That's why the deceiver continually whispers lies about who we are, who God is, God's heart toward us, and the intimacy God wants us to share with Him. Satan employs a three-part strategy to steal, kill, and destroy. The strategy looks like this:

- **First things first:** In the normal course of every person's life, things happen that hurt us, shame us, or cause us to be afraid. The more severe these events, the greater their impact can be.

- **A wounded heart:** The pain we experience causes a wound. If left untreated with healing or restoration, infection sets in. Infection comes in the form of feelings of rejection, lack of self-worth, or worse, feelings of self-hatred. We respond to such feelings with hopelessness, depression, or abusing substances or people.

- **A whispered lie:** The enemy of life begins to whisper lies in your ear. If you don't have a voice of truth to offset the lies of the evil one, you begin to believe the lies. As time goes by, you even begin to speak the lies out as truth: no one loves me; I am a nobody; I am all alone; I deserve this treatment; it was my fault. Most of all, we begin to believe "people will never accept me," and "God will never forgive me."

All too often, Satan succeeds in building in us a distorted view of God and the world. At that point, the enemy has won. He then has control of our thoughts. Our thoughts in turn control our actions. We have fallen into his trap.

No wonder Proverbs 4:23 instructs, "Above all else, guard your heart, for it is the wellspring of life" (NIV). Jesus clearly described how powerful the core beliefs of our hearts become in directing our lives and our legacies. "It is what comes from inside that defiles you. For from within, out of a person's heart, come evil thoughts" (Mark 7:20–21).

The battle of life happens mostly inside you and me, in our minds. We have an enemy who fights dirty, and our secrets give him ammunition. He proves more than happy to use our secrets against us. So one of the most practical things any of us can do is to break the silence. When we open our secrets to the light of shared truth, we literally take out of the devil's hands the stick he has been using to beat us black and blue.

So how do we break the silence and get free? How do we overcome years and years of enemy strongholds over our thoughts, beliefs, and lives? The answer scares us terribly. We need to tell our story.

We need to speak out the hurts and pain. We need to expose the darkness to the light. This step has a purpose far beyond reopening old wounds. In an amazing way, honesty builds community. God never intended us to struggle alone. People need each other, and we were designed for strong relationships. Amazing things occur when two or more people grasp hands and hearts and share their pain together. God is in their midst. He does amazing things with those who are humble and open to His supernatural surgery of the heart. Through God's power, we find recovery, freedom, and healing.

Solomon, the wisest human king ever, described our need for each other in the book of Ecclesiastes. He said a person without a companion experiences "no end" of struggles. "Two are better than one because they have a good reward for their efforts. For if either falls, his companion can lift him up; but pity the one who falls without another to lift him up. Also, if two lie down together, they can keep warm; but how can one person alone keep warm? And if somebody overpowers one person, two can resist him. A cord of three strands is not easily broken" (Ecclesiastes 4:9–12, HCSB).

We all need someone we trust and with whom we can share our story. We need someone who will listen and not judge. We need someone who will keep our story confidential and who will pray with and for us. The more shameful our past seems, the more desperate the need.

Because the thought of surrendering our secret shame frightens us so, we need to consider what disclosure does and does not mean. I am not suggesting that transparency means telling everyone everything. Healthy boundaries mean we disclose ourselves appropriately to the right people, in the right way, at the right time. It most definitely does not mean we open ourselves to unsafe people.

A daunting problem for many of us is how to find the safe person or group where we can share our pain. Sometimes we don't even know what a safe person looks like. We need someone who will know all about us and love us still. We need others who will both love us unconditionally and tell us the truth.

If you already have that kind of relationship, you're a fortunate person. You're in a distinct and blessed minority. Many people desperately long for such deep relationships. If you are like most of us, you will have to seek out that kind of support.

Many of us have found great benefit from seeking a safe place to share our experiences through specialized groups outside of our regular friends. A homogenous group of people who have shared similar experiences can hear our story with understanding. In a purely pragmatic sense, openness with strangers can simply be easier. Many churches offer counseling and support for both men and women.

I know in my particular situation, I was absolutely terrified by the thought of being found out. I chose abortion in the first place to keep my immorality a secret.

Fear continues to be one reason many women continue to guard their secrets. In the process we've fallen for a great deception.

Who do we really protect by holding onto secrets? We cover up the deceiver's lie that our past abuse, rejection, abandonment, and sin hasn't hurt us. Remaining silent keeps us in the darkness of the lie, but freedom comes in exposing it.

Please understand, God's desire is not to expose you, leaving you feeling alone and vulnerable. Rather, God knows that our confession exposes the darkness to the light. Once in the light, God can do His healing work. You have a protecting and caring Father who covers His children with grace, not shame. Be courageous; under the protection of God, expose the enemy.

Let Me Go First and Show You the Way

Not long after becoming a believer in Christ, I began to sense God calling me to share my story with my new Christian friends. As a new believer, I couldn't imagine why God was bringing me down this path in my new life with Him. Why was He asking me to share that, of all things? I had, after all, just started a new future in Him. I had just asked Christ into my heart at a woman's retreat. I had made all new Christian friends and was changing all of the things about my life that I knew should be changed.

I knew I had a ways to go. I'd come to the end of myself and given my life to Jesus in a big, fat mess. My marriage had been in shambles. My kids were being thrown back and forth between my husband and me. My job was filled with dishonesty and immorality. I had a lot to get right. In the middle of these present problems, I couldn't imagine why God would have me concentrating on something that had happened seven years earlier. Weren't we supposed to forget the past and concentrate on the future?

I had never talked to anyone about my past. It was a secret, something I barely remembered myself. Yet I had no doubt God was leading me. I called one of my new Bible study girlfriends and asked her to meet me for lunch.

My heart pounded in my chest, and my head was spinning. My friend Ann, with her sparkling smile, was bounding toward me from the tearoom parking lot. No getting away this time, it was too late to duck. Ann instinctively reached for my hands as I began to tremble, and tears ran down my cheeks. I had never been so scared in my life.

Ann was my new best friend. She first approached me at

the church ladies' retreat. She had invested in me, pulling me into her circle of beautiful, godly women, and coaching me in my new walk with God. Ann was the person who taught me how to pray out loud. She was the one who planted within me a hunger for the Bible and a desire for intimacy with God. She continued to walk with me step-by-step through the metamorphosis into my new life in Jesus.

In the few months that had passed since I surrendered my life to God at that ladies' retreat, my life had turned around so beautifully. My marriage, my children, even my music had been transformed by the new life Jesus offers. My spirit and emotions had gone from depression to hopeful. Little did I suspect that this incredible walk into new life with God would lead me to a crossroad where I found myself face-to-face with a dark secret from my old life. Not only had I hidden this secret from the world but I had stuffed it so deep inside that I was hiding it from myself.

As I clutched Ann's hands that day at the tearoom, I felt like my newly found peace and joy was about to be demolished, but I knew God was asking me to surrender my secret, just as He'd asked that I surrender my life to Him.

Although I dreaded it, I had to tell Ann my story. The secrets swelled so fiercely in my heart that I was about to burst. Turmoil and panic gripped my chest because I had no idea what Ann would say or how exposing the darkness of my past would affect our friendship. Ann and all my new friends at church seemed so godly and good. What would they think of me? What would they think about the awful things I had done?

Action Step Two: What's Your Story?

Friend, you've made a huge step today by reading this far. I'll share more of what happened later. First, let's stop and process this a bit, shall we?

What do you think might happen if your friends and family knew some of the secrets of your past?

How does it feel to read about the patterns we fall into that allow Satan to distort our view and build walls around our true self?

Using my example above, write your story. Don't worry about grammar or writing style—this is meant for your eyes only.

Join me on my website at www.patlayton.net for additional resources.

Step Three: Confronting the Truth

God's Word is quite clear about the power of truth. John 8:32 says: "You will know the truth and the truth will set you free"!

In step one, we discussed the process of deception Satan uses to rob us of freedom and an abundant life. The Bible calls the devil the father of lies. Satan continues to pour his twisted deceptions into our world. God knows how lies provide Satan his best ammunition. When we fall for and then perpetrate deceit, bit by bit we take on the character of the evil one.

God hates lies for at least two reasons. They represent the exact opposite of His character, and they hurt those He loves. Scripture makes clear God's opinion of all things false: "Lying lips are detestable to the LORD, but faithful people are His delight" (Proverbs 12:22, HCSB).

Proverbs 6:16–19 says the Lord hates six things, "haughty eyes, a lying tongue, hands that shed innocent blood, a heart that devises wicked schemes, feet that are quick to rush into evil, a false witness who pours out lies and a man who stirs up dissension among brothers" (NIV).

God didn't put those statements in His Word to make us miserable or to control us. He seeks to guide and protect us by setting boundaries for our own good. We learned from John 8:32

that the truth will set us free.

No lie ever has, or ever will, bring freedom.

Whether people lie for their own gain, to protect themselves, or because they have personally bought into the deception, lies cause serious damage. The power of a lie bears fruit when we will act on it as truth.

Lies have eroded truth many places in our world. We have built a world culture very much like the one described in Jeremiah 9: "They make ready their tongue like a bow, to shoot lies. ... They go from one sin to another; they do not acknowledge me, declares the LORD. Everyone has to be on guard against his friend. Don't trust any brother, for every brother will certainly deceive, and every friend spread slander. Each one betrays his friend; no one tells the truth" (vv. 3–5, HCSB).

To find freedom we must build a microcosm of truth out of this world of deception. We begin that process in our relationship to God and with at least one trustworthy fellow human.

If, like me, you face the aftermath of a past filled with regrets and loss, consider the circumstances that led to some of your pain. Regardless of whether or not your heartbreak was caused by your own bad choices, like most of mine were, or if you were the innocent victim of someone else's sin, what messages did you hear? How did those closest to you respond to your needs and pain? As part of healing, we must look at what we believed about the brokenness of our past and begin to understand some of the effects that may have followed.

Where Do We Find Truth?

However, I have good news for you, my sister. There is someone who knows all about your past and still loves you just the same.

Look with me at another part of Psalm 139:

O LORD, you have searched me
  and you know me.
You know when I sit and when I rise;
  you perceive my thoughts from afar.
You discern my going out and my lying down;
  you are familiar with all my ways.
Before a word is on my tongue
  you know it completely, O LORD.
You hem me in—behind and before;
  you have laid your hand upon me.
Such knowledge is too wonderful for me,
  too lofty for me to attain.
Where can I go from your Spirit?
  Where can I flee from your presence?
If I go up to the heavens, you are there;
  if I make my bed in the depths, you are there.
If I rise on the wings of the dawn,
  if I settle on the far side of the sea,
even there your hand will guide me,
  your right hand will hold me fast.
If I say, "Surely the darkness will hide me
  and the light become night around me,"
even the darkness will not be dark to you;
  the night will shine like the day,
  for darkness is as light to you.

Psalm 139:1–12, NIV

Nothing is hidden from God's sight. He is with you during the darkest, loneliest, and most difficult times of your life. God sees with complete clarity in the darkness of your soul and your deep secrets. God never leaves you.

God sees and knows your feelings of guilt, shame, depression, regret, and anger. He has seen the days of your struggles with feelings of unworthiness, fear, numbness, and lack of trust. Maybe there have been times in your life when you have turned to substance abuse and other destructive behavior to mask or numb your feelings of pain or failure. Perhaps some of these emotions or actions seem familiar. You may have never connected the dots and realized that your feelings could be a result of you holding so much bottled inside. Keeping us from understanding the cause and effect of loneliness, depression, or just feeling "stuck" represents just another way the enemy deceives women.

In another place, the psalmist wrote, "When I kept silent about my sin, my body wasted away through my groaning all day long. For day and night your hand was heavy upon me, my vitality was drained away as with the fever heat of summer" (Psalm 32:3–4, NASB).

Praise God! However, the psalmist didn't only describe the problem. He continued to the healing solution, "I acknowledged my sin to you and my iniquity I did not hide. I said, 'I will confess my transgressions to the LORD: and you forgave the guilt of my sin'" (Psalm 32: 5, NASB).

According to this passage, when we stay silent regarding our sin, our bodies waste away, and our energy literally drains away. Secrets can play havoc on a person's physical, emotional, mental, and spiritual well-being. We can't allow ourselves to stop with that loss. God wants to heal our hearts and use our stories to help others. Confession leads to forgiveness and peace.

Several times we've looked at God's promises of truth, hope, and redemption. The other remedies we've used as an attempt to relieve our pain trap us in dark places. When we have tried self-destructive remedies like drugs, alcohol, and meaningless relationships, we always end up just as empty as ever. You may be reading this book because you've already discovered you can't find your way out of those dark places alone.

Rescue begins when we acknowledge that we are powerless to heal our lives on our own. Only the Savior can rescue, re-create, and restore us from the inside out. We've discussed how, if we want to experience healing, we must be willing to trust Jesus to take us on the unfamiliar and risky path to it.

God created us in His image (Genesis 1:27) with the freedom of choice. Since the moment Adam and Eve chose to disobey God, the world has been anything but paradise. Our freedom to choose has destroyed life across the ages, but God willingly created us with the free will to make our own decisions. We always have free choice, but choices always have consequences.

Before entering the Promised Land, Moses challenged the Israelites, saying, "Today I have given you the choice between life and death, between blessings and curses. Now I call on heaven and earth to witness the choice you make. Oh, that you would choose life, so that you and your descendants might live" (Deuteronomy 30:19, NLT).

Will you reject the past with its shame, curses, and death, choosing instead the path to life, freedom, and blessing with

Jesus? Will you choose life?

This can be an overwhelming chapter. You may be reading these truths for the first time. New feelings may be starting to stir inside you, and you may begin to feel angry. That is to be expected. The next chapter will deal with the emotion of anger; sometimes anger is exactly what we need to feel!

Action Step Three: Consider the *Truth* about Your Heartbreak

Take some time for prayer and reflection. Ask God to help you get a deeper insight into all you have considered in this section. You may have encountered a lot of new information. Give God time to show you His heart for you as you proceed toward the complete healing He wants for His daughters. God may show you how you have allowed the enemy's lies to push you around. He also may show you how you have been affected by secrets and lies even when trying to protect yourself from well-meaning friends, family, or the church.

As you reflect on your journey, let me suggest some clarifying questions to ask yourself. These questions will help to think through aspects of your situation.

When you ask God a question, expect His Spirit to respond to your heart. Be careful not to rush it or manufacture an answer. Don't turn the Bible into a reference book or spiritual encyclopedia. Just pose the question to God and wait on Him. The litmus test for anything we hear from God is alignment with the Bible as our ultimate truth source.

The following questions ask you to look into your heart and consider with brutal honesty your deepest feelings and beliefs. Remember, our behaviors are the best indicators of what we really believe in our innermost being (Psalm 51:6). Be sure to capture your insights and feelings.

Questions to Ask of Myself

What lies do I still hold on to that prevent me from feeling the full impact of true freedom in Christ?

What lies have I used to protect myself? To protect others?

What do I fear might happen if I let truth surface in my life?

Questions to Ask of God

Your Word says that you can see me, Lord. Why do You allow something like what I have endured when You know how much it will hurt?

Why didn't you stop me?

Where were You?

Extra Steps

Often, we embrace limiting beliefs about our past heartache. We feel isolated and alone. Now might be a great time to contact a biblical counselor for some fresh perspective on the particular heartache you have endured. It is *critical* for us to understand the nature of our heartbreak and exactly how widespread and more common than we realize this heartache might be.

Seek wise counsel and support and allow God to work this out in you once and forever.

Join me on my website at www.patlayton.net for additional resources.

Step Four: Don't Drink the Poison

When we take the time to understand truth, feelings of anger often result.

Truth means facing the facts, often facts we would rather keep avoiding. Truth means we shed the false comfort of believing what we wish were real.

In my case, nothing was true.

I struggled to open my eyes. Although I could hear soft whispers of unknown words in the room, I could not move my body or speak past the tube running down my throat. I couldn't remember where I was or how I got there. Within moments, I wished I had not awakened at all.

My newly wedded husband and my parents kept a stoic vigil at my hospital bed, as I was struggling to regain consciousness.

As tiny bits of my body and my mind began to regain feeling, a flood of anger rushed into each space. Now, I remember.

The people at the hospital said that the whole procedure would be over in thirty minutes.

They said I would be picking up my five-year-old son from school that afternoon. They said a few aspirin would do the trick after the procedure.

Nothing they said was true.

The choice I was making that day was supposed to be a three-hour break in my busy day, allowing me to go on with my life by noon. Instead, I had an allergic reaction to the anesthesia they used to put me to sleep, and they had to put me on a respirator to keep me alive. By noon, I was still unable to breathe on my own, much less pick up my son from school. My new husband was forced to call on my parents to do that for us. Of course, after picking our son up from school, my parents had rushed to the hospital.

The people at the clinic had said no one would even have to know. They said there was "no need to worry" about the fever and the cramps that lasted five days after I went home from the hospital. As I grew worse, they changed their minds and said, "During the emergency we encountered during your first procedure, parts of the fetus were left behind. We will need to repeat the procedure."

I never even thought about the word *fetus* until they said it. After that, all I could think was "baby." My baby. "Parts" left behind? Which "parts"? The heart? The hands? The parts of a boy or of a girl? My God, which parts?

How about your story? Do you see some lies that were told? Have you endured some unkept promises? Was there a relationship that turned out to be something other than what you believed?

Allowing ourselves to look at the *truth* about our past heartbreak and get angry, whether it is uncovering the facts about abuse, online perversion, the results of alcoholism on a family member who (dot, dot, dot . . . fill in your loss) may be the primary path to freedom.

The Power of Anger

Anger is an extremely powerful emotion. Most of the time we view it as a negative part of ourselves that should be denied or at least controlled. The truth is, God created all our emotions for our benefit—including anger. However, when we don't use emotions properly, we can do a great deal of damage both to ourselves and others. Let's talk about anger—the good, the bad, and the ugly.

The Bible has much to say about how to handle our emotions the right way. A verse in Ephesians shows us that anger isn't necessarily a sin. It instructs us to lay aside falsehood and, "speak the truth each of you with his neighbor, for we are all members of one another. Be angry, and yet do not sin" (Ephesians 4:25–26, NASB).

What? Did the Bible just give us permission to be angry? Anger is a God-given emotion and is not a sin. How we deal with our anger may be either wholesome or sinful. Anger becomes dangerous and destructive when we react to it in ways that hurt ourselves and others.

Think of unmanaged anger as being like the acid in your car battery. In the right container and used for the right purpose, the acid provides power to start your car. In the wrong container, anger becomes corrosive and destructive to whatever it contacts.

God gave you the ability to feel anger as a motive force. When we encounter false and hurtful things, anger motivates us to change them. But anger has a short useful shelf life. If we hold on to our anger for weeks, months, or years, then it can overtake our lives and consume who we are. As the anger corrodes our soul, every thought, every action can become motivated by anger and the resulting bitterness. The person God created us to be ends up buried deep beneath anger, with resentment and bitterness piled on top.

The words, "be angry" in Ephesians 4:26 is in the Greek imperative tense used for commands or direct instructions. Shockingly, to those of us who have learned to deny and stuff our anger, in this passage God actually commands us to be angry. Two excellent examples in the Bible illustrate God's command.

Moses was an Israelite slave in Egypt whom God miraculously spared from slaughter through his mother's great courage and sacrifice. God raised Moses into a position of great influence in Pharaoh's household, but the events of one day changed all that. The book of Exodus tells the story as follows:

> Years later, after Moses had grown up, he went out to his own people and observed their forced labor. He saw an Egyptian beating a Hebrew, one of his people. Looking all around and seeing no

one, he struck the Egyptian dead and hid him in the sand. The next day he went out and saw two Hebrews fighting. He asked the one in the wrong, "Why are you attacking your neighbor?" "Who made you a leader and judge over us?" the man replied. "Are you planning to kill me as you killed the Egyptian?" Then Moses became afraid and thought: What I did is certainly known. When Pharaoh heard about this, he tried to kill Moses. But Moses fled from Pharaoh and went to live in the land of Midian.

Exodus 2:11-15, HCSB

Moses became angry when he saw how Egyptians were treating the Hebrews—his people. His anger was justified. What was not justified was allowing that anger to spill over into killing the Egyptian. Moses's sin was not being angry but committing murder. His response to anger was not healthy or constructive in solving Israel's problem. It actually made things worse and resulted in Moses having to flee the country. Moses should have and could have channeled his anger in more constructive ways.

In another example, Fredrick Douglass was a slave in the pre–Civil War south. After escaping slavery, he became an abolitionist leader, author, and orator, greatly influencing the efforts to outlaw slavery. Douglass channeled his anger in constructive ways. The result contributed to freedom for millions and changed history.

Jesus provides us another example of anger in the Bible. When He saw how temple businessmen were cheating and extorting people who came to the temple to worship God, Jesus too demonstrated anger.

> Jesus entered the Temple and began to drive out all the people buying and selling animals for sacrifice. He knocked over the tables of the moneychangers and the chairs of those selling doves. He said to them, "The Scriptures declare, 'My Temple will be called a house of prayer,' but you have turned it into a den of thieves!"
>
> Matthew 21:10–13, NLT

Jesus responded differently to anger. Jesus did not destructively hurt anyone. Yes, He made a mess, but Jesus channeled His anger for a purpose. He was angry at how the people of Jerusalem were treating the temple. They had turned a holy place into a market, a place where people were taking advantage of others, and a place of business, not worship. His actions were instructive and corrective. In the process, He definitely ruffled some feathers and possibly raised a few welts.

Of course, as the Son of God, Jesus was better able to judge the degree of action to take with His anger. I'm not recommending we take a bullwhip to the person in the overpriced kiosk at the mall. The offense Jesus faced was serious. His reaction was measured and proportional.

From Jesus's cleansing of the temple, we can see that physically expressing anger can be justified under some circumstances. Such righteous anger must be neither a means to selfish gain nor a way to hurt someone. Acting on anger may be justified when it results in a change and makes the world a better place. Godly anger aligns us with the emotion God feels when people are abused.

As women, we sometimes have to deal with a great deal of anger. The challenge is to sort through that anger and express it in healthy and constructive ways. For each of us, dealing with anger will be different, but it has some common elements.

To Implode or Explode?

Are you an imploder or an exploder when it comes to anger? Dr. Gary Chapman describes two unhealthy ways of managing anger: holding it in or expressing it with aggressive behaviors. Implosive anger is internalized anger that we never outwardly express. You might hear, "I'm not angry, just frustrated" or "I'm not mad, just disappointed" as two common expressions of an imploder.

Since so many of us have been taught to deny our anger, we do well to examine the previously cited Bible passage from Ephesians a little more closely.

The apostle Paul wrote:

> Therefore, laying aside falsehood, speak the truth each one of you with his neighbor, for we are members of one another. Be angry, and yet do not sin; do not let the sun go down on your anger, and do not give the devil an opportunity. He who steals must steal no longer; but rather he must labor, performing with his own hands what is good, so that he will have something to share with

one who has need. Let no unwholesome word proceed from your mouth, but only such a word as is good for edification according to the need of the moment, so that it will give grace to those who hear. Do not grieve the Holy Spirit of God, by whom you were sealed for the day of redemption. Let all bitterness and wrath and anger and clamor and slander be put away from you, along with all malice. Be kind to one another, tenderhearted, forgiving each other, just as God in Christ also has forgiven you.

Ephesians 4:25–32, NASB

The apostle says that unexpressed or bottled-up anger gives the devil an opportunity in our lives, grieving the Holy Spirit, and giving bitterness, wrath, anger, clamor, slander, and malice a foothold. In verse 29, the word *unwholesome* means *rotten*. Anger can lead to rottenness if we allow it to fester. It eventually will consume all that we do and all that we are. The end product of such stuffed anger becomes bitterness and unforgiveness.

To be human means occasional anger, but haven't we all known people for whom bitterness has become more than a passing phase? We can think of bitterness as the ossified form of anger. When we don't deal with our anger, it gradually petrifies. If we continue to bury our anger, we risk becoming like a person dragging around the skeleton of a long-dead dinosaur. Unforgiveness weighs down our lives. It saps our strength and poisons our character.

Implosive anger has to find expression somehow, so it results in passive-aggressive behavior, displaced anger, physiological and emotional stress, resentment, bitterness, and hatred. Imploders typically keep score, so living with one always carries the potential for a delayed explosion from a dormant volcano.

When Paul advised, "Do not let the sun go down on your anger," he wasn't dealing in religious platitudes. He was warning us to deal with our anger promptly and effectively before it spreads and does more damage. He also warned, "Do not give the devil an opportunity." Paul explained that poorly managed anger offers the devil a *topos* —the Greek word from which we get *topography*. It means a plot of land.

Imagine that you are fighting a war—because you are by the way. The last thing you would want would be to freely grant your enemy a military base from which to launch more attacks into your life and relationships. When you put anger in your refrigerator and save it for tomorrow, you grant your enemy that forward operating base. He will prove more than willing to lob mortar shells at you from the location you've allowed.

Implosive anger takes an emotion God built into each of us and makes it a self-destructive internal source of conflict. It may pop up at any time and always in the unhealthiest way. Interestingly enough, we can practice both implosive anger and the opposite as well. Sometimes we toggle back and forth from imploding to exploding.

Explosive anger is the other unhealthy, ungodly management technique. We may manifest it as uncontrolled fury in a verbal and/or physical form. According to Ephesians 4:31 the outcome of all poorly managed anger is bitterness, wrath, more anger, clamor, slander, and malice.

Explosive anger verbally attacks by screaming, cursing, condemning, name-calling, humiliating, or threatening. It damages the self-esteem of both the giver and the recipient. Ultimately, it destroys relationships because the exploder causes the anger recipient to retreat for emotional safety. Exploders frequently blame their victims for "making them mad," or they minimize their outbursts by labeling them "blowing off steam." In extreme cases, the exploder may grab, push, or strike in anger. All unhealthy anger is harmful, but physical abuse should not be tolerated.

A Healthy Alternative

Like water in a leaky container, unresolved anger never remains confined. It always finds some unhealthy way to express itself. Gary Chapman, author of *The Five Languages of Apology*, says, "When one's sense of right is violated, that person will experience anger. He or she will feel wronged and resentful at the person (or persons) who have violated."

We girls often react to things in ways we don't understand. We find ourselves overreacting to events and circumstances in ways we don't expect—sometimes with anger, or other times with great sadness or hurt. Now that you are on your healing journey, you can begin to make sense of these uncomfortable emotions.

Often, we hesitate to admit our anger toward others for fear of rejection. We find ourselves defending those we feel we should love. In order to heal, it's important to acknowledge anger and release it in a healthy way.

Action Step Four: Ephesians Anger Checklist

Based on many women's experiences and the Ephesians passage, we have assembled a checklist to help you in evaluating and dealing with anger issues. Consider your responses to these areas and questions:

1. Assess Your Primary Emotion: Does your anger stem from loss of control,   hurt, or indignation about wrongs?

2, Take Off Your Mask: What has hurt you? Talk through your feelings   (Ephesians 4:25–26).

3. Deal with Issues and Confront: Have you learned to communicate issues clearly and early? Be sure the goal is resolving issues, not getting back at people (Ephesians 4:28).

4. Don't Let Anger Fester and Rot: Do you have unresolved anger? Buried anger scribbles a written invitation to the enemy to exploit us in wounding others and ourselves (Ephesians 4:29).

5. God Cares Deeply about Your Anger: Ask yourself, *"Have I turned my anger over to God?"* His heart aches when we allow rages, resentment, or bitterness to take root and grow (Ephesians 4:30).

6. Replace Anger with Forgiveness and Compassion: Have you received the forgiveness God offers? Have you extended that forgiveness to others? Because God has forgiven us so much; we need to be willing to forgive others (Ephesians 4:32).

How about your story? Do you see some lies that were told? Some unkept promises? Was there a relationship that turned out to be something other than what you believed?

Are there some specific people you need help forgiving?

Print out the Ephesians anger checklist and do your best to answer every question honestly. If you have a close friend, family member, or mentor to share the list with, that is even better.

This is a critical step to healing, so take the time to let God work it out in your heart!

Join me on my website at www.patlayton.net for additional resources.

Step Five: Taste the Freedom

The process of working through anger can be exhausting. The next part of the journey to freedom from the past, is to release anger and lighten the load of this heavy burden you've been carrying. The goal of this chapter is to start moving from anger toward forgiveness.

As you begin to let go of your anger, remember it is you who is being healed. Release the burden of resentment to God and allow Him to set you free. The truth is that holding on to anger and unforgiveness is like drinking poison and waiting for someone else to die from its effects. In the previous chapter, you took a look at the truth about anger. To become angry is a normal response when we examine the "free choice" of our heartbreak.

As we saw in the last chapter, anger can be good. It can get things done. Anger can get our attention and result in action. One caveat always applies to anger, however. The energy it generates must be channeled and directed. Untamed anger just lashes out at random. We must learn and discipline ourselves to guide its reactive energy to helpful ends. Then results can include change and restoration. Before we can express anger as a positive, we will look at the healing that comes from not only letting go of our damaging anger but forgiving those who have hurt us.

In step three, you may have considered some people involved in your past pain or losses. Those may include people you really love, or at least *want* to love. You may find yourself saying, "I want to stop being angry, but I just can't". I'd like to gently remind you. *If you want to experience true healing, at some point you have to make a decision to let go of your anger.* The truth is, God wants us to go a step further: He wants us to forgive. In an area of our lives where we have been so hurt, it's difficult to imagine forgiving some of our offenders. However, with God's grace it is possible.

In referring to His people, God says, "I will forgive their wickedness and will remember their sins no more" (Jeremiah 31:34, NIV). According to Jeremiah, God forgives us completely. His example points us to a key element—what forgiveness does not entail. *Before we can define genuine forgiveness and make a case for its necessity in healing, first we need to clarify what forgiveness is not.*

- *Forgiveness is* not *forgetting.* We frequently hear the phrase "forgive and forget," but forgiveness does not imply amnesia. When the Bible says that God "will remember their sins no more," it doesn't mean that He suddenly has no recollection of an offense. God does not develop a kind of heavenly Alzheimer's. It means that God chooses not to catalog our sins and use the information against us. God chooses to pass over His right to hold our wrongs against us.

- *Forgiveness is* not *minimizing the hurt.* Forgiveness does not water down the offense by saying something like, "It's okay, it wasn't that bad." Or

52

"I know that you didn't mean to hurt me." The truth is, you've been hurt deeply, and sometimes, intentionally. Forgiveness does not say, "I'm all right; it's just a flesh wound" when real trauma is involved. Instead, forgiveness calls the violation what it is just as an umpire calls what he sees.

- *Forgiveness does* not *necessarily mean reconciliation.* Perhaps you were thinking, "If I forgive my ex-husband and my parents, then I have to initiate or at least be receptive to reconciliation." Hear this truth: forgiveness and reconciliation are two separate issues. Keep them apart. We definitely need to forgive for many reasons. We choose to reconcile or not to reconcile—and to what degree we reconcile—based on the facts of our situations.

  Truthfully, you may actually desire reconciliation and would give anything for it to happen, but reconciliation isn't even on the radar screen of some of the people involved in your past. Some people are unsafe for us, and we most definitely should keep our distance from them. In some cases, the very thought of required reconciliation feels like being sentenced to life in prison without parole. Forgiveness recognizes that reconciliation may be neither possible nor wise.

  Relationships, and therefore reconciliation, are also matters of degree. Forgiving someone doesn't require becoming best friends or even close acquaintances with him or her. In some cases, you can genuinely forgive without ever initiating a relationship. In other cases, you may reconcile a relationship while maintaining your distance for any of a plethora of reasons. At times, you may even find great love and support through reconciliation.

Some of these concepts or definitions may alter your view of forgiveness. You may find yourself more open to forgive when you dispense with wrong concepts of forgiveness.

The Bible tells a wonderful story about a young man who had every reason to hate and hold a grudge. He even had a delicious opportunity to experience the joy of a "payback," but he chose a different response.

Joseph's story begins in Genesis 37 and goes for ten chapters. You may want to take time to read it in its entirety before continuing to let God show you the way to redemptive healing.

Joseph was favored by his father but alienated from his brothers. When he was only seventeen, his brothers plotted to kill him but then tempered their actions by selling him into slavery. Thus, he found himself a slave in the foreign kingdom of Egypt.

After years spent as a slave, Joseph was imprisoned for a crime he didn't commit. For thirteen years, he faced shame and rejection. Through a series of divine interventions, Joseph left prison and became the second ruler of Egypt, reporting directly to Pharaoh. Ironically, he found himself facing the very brothers who wronged him, with them in great need of his help.

To add to the drama, Joseph framed his brothers as thieves, and they did not recognize him. Joseph held in his hands the very thing for which bitter people everywhere long. He had all the power. Joseph could pay his brothers back. Unlimited revenge was within his grasp. His brothers didn't even know that Joseph could understand their language. With the brothers trembling in fear, Joseph . . . well, let's just read the account directly from Genesis 45, shall we?

Joseph could no longer keep his composure in front of all his attendants, so he called out, "Send everyone away from me!" No one was with him when he revealed his identity to his brothers. But he wept so loudly that the Egyptians heard it, and also Pharaoh's household heard it. Joseph said to his brothers, "I am Joseph! Is my father still living?" But his brothers were too terrified to answer him. Then Joseph said to his brothers, "Please, come near me," and they came near. "I am Joseph, your brother," he said, "the one you sold into Egypt. And now don't be worried or angry with yourselves for selling me here, because God sent me ahead of you to preserve life. For the famine has been in the land these two years, and there will be five more years without plowing or harvesting. God sent me ahead of you to establish you as a remnant within the land and to keep you alive by a great deliverance. Therefore, it was not you who sent me here, but God. He has made me a father to Pharaoh, lord of his entire household, and ruler over all the land of Egypt."

Genesis 45:1–8, HCSB

Joseph's brothers were terrified when they recognized him. After selling him into slavery, they never imagined that he would be second in command in Egypt. For all they knew, he was dead.

Joseph's perspective about God enabled him to forgive his brothers. He saw God's hand in everything that happened. Being sold into slavery resulted in his chance to save the lives of his father and his brothers.

Joseph had every reason and opportunity to repay his brothers for the agony they caused him. Joseph, however, did not choose to take that opportunity. He forgave them because he'd allowed love to replace bitterness and because he'd learned the truth the apostle Paul later expressed in Romans 8:28. Joseph understood that "God causes all things to work together for good to those who love God, to those who are called according to His purpose" (Romans 8:28, NASB).

The New Testament, of course, further enforces the need to forgive. A man came to Jesus and asked how many times he had to forgive his brother. Matthew 18 records Jesus's response with a story. Jesus described a man who owed a vast amount of money. The holder of his debt decided to have the man and his entire family thrown in a debtor's prison, but the man begged for leniency. The master forgave the massive debt, and the man promptly accosted another man who owed him a small debt. When the master heard what the forgiven debtor had done, he summoned him and said, "'You wicked slave! I forgave you all that debt because you begged me. Shouldn't you also have had mercy on your fellow slave as I had mercy on you?'" (Matthew 18:32–33).

As the consummate rabbi, Jesus knew the most powerful

way to teach is to lay out the truth and allow the hearers to make the connections for themselves. In the story of the debtor, the underlying question is how we can be so petty as to refuse to forgive the relatively small debt of what others have done to us when God has forgiven us the massive wrong of our sin? If even the most sinned-against among us would pile up all the wrongs they have endured, could the list ever compare to what the perfect and totally innocent Son of God suffered?

God requires us to forgive anyone who offends us. He does not give us the option to choose whom we'll forgive and against whom we will continue to hold a grudge. Paul wrote: "Make allowance for each other's faults and forgive anyone who offends you. Remember, the Lord forgave you, so you must forgive others" (Colossians 3:13, NLT).

God commands us to forgive for His glory, for the healing of others, and for our own benefit. Forgiveness helps maintain harmony in relationships. It also creates deep peace and joy in the lives of the two captives it sets free—your offender and you!

As a woman who has faced some pain and loneliness of the past, you have a reason to be angry with many people. You may have justifiable reasons to be angry and cheated by some of your loved ones and your circumstances.

True forgiveness is seldom easy. It can be quite costly, but it offers us a powerful weapon for tearing down strongholds in our lives and hearts. The enemy uses unforgiveness and anger to keep us in bondage. When we surrender our unforgiveness and anger, we set our own hearts free, so God can take us places we never dreamed possible.

However, a number of barriers can hinder a person from

letting go of anger and interfering in the healing process. A few examples include:

- If I forgive the offender, he or she will never understand the severity of the act.
- If I forgive, I will look weak; I have my pride.
- He or she doesn't deserve forgiveness, only punishment. I can't let him or her off the hook.
- Forgiveness isn't possible for this (what was done to me was unforgivable).
- The offender shows no remorse, so I have no responsibility to forgive.
- If I let go of my anger, I may also let go of my loss.
- Letting go of anger means letting go of my relationships with persons involved in my pain (sometimes anger is the only emotion connecting people).
- I'm comfortable with the status quo, and I'm afraid of the unknowns that will come.

Benefits and Consequences of Forgiveness:

We often believe the lie that our anger effectively punishes the offender. The truth is, we are the only one undergoing punishment. We punish ourselves and are imprisoned by it.

Frederick Buechner writes in *Wishful Thinking:*

Of the Seven Deadly Sins, anger is possibly the most fun. To lick your wounds, to smack your lips over grievances long past, to roll over your tongues the prospect of bitter confrontations still to come, to savor to the last toothsome morsel both the pain you are given and the pain you are giving back-—in many ways it is a feast fit for a king. The chief drawback is that what you are wolfing down is yourself. The skeleton at the feast is you. When we choose to forgive, we release our prisoner from the dungeon and discover that we are subsequently freed from the dank cell of our own bitterness. Spiritually and emotionally, forgiveness frees us.

In Genesis 50:20, Joseph told his brothers, "You intended to harm me, but God intended it for good to accomplish what is now being done, the saving of many lives" (NIV). You may not even imagine being able to say these words.

Forgiving Yourself

Many people in our culture talk about forgiving ourselves. Women commonly feel that while God has forgiven us, we cannot seem to forgive ourselves. We need to grasp a crucial truth that may surprise many. God never intended for us to forgive ourselves. The Bible does not identify the need to forgive ourselves. In fact, I don't think we are capable of it.

The key is not forgiving yourself but accepting God's forgiveness. When we try to forgive ourselves, we seek to do God's work in His place. The distinction may trouble you and seem like semantics, but it goes to the very heart of the Scripture and the Gospel. Let me try to explain with two biblical examples.

In the Garden of Eden, God gave our first human parents a division of labor—not between Adam and Eve but between the pair and God. They were to take care of the tasks He gave them—tend the garden, populate the earth, that sort of human stuff. God was to take care of the God stuff. But in Genesis 3, Satan came and tempted Eve with the thought that God was holding out on them. If they would just disobey God and make their own decisions (eat the fruit), they would become "like God, knowing good and evil."

For millennia, theologians have debated and tried to describe the heart of Eve and Adam's sin. They use *pride* and other terms, but this much is certain—Eve wanted to have what God had and to take over His place.

"What does that have to do with forgiving?" you may ask. In the same way, forgiving is God's territory, not ours. Only He is holy. All sin may hurt us, but it is ultimately against Him. Only He has the infinite power to forgive. When we push Him aside like a petulant preschooler and say, "Me do it," we only interfere with the process.

Allow me a second biblical illustration from the Gospel. The Gospel is the good news that Christ has died for our sins, to do for us what we could never do for ourselves. The Gospel means much more than simply forgiveness, but it certainly means no less.

Ephesians 2 underscores the glorious fact that the Gospel is a gift. "For by grace you are saved through faith, and this is not from yourselves; it is God's gift— not from works, so that no one can boast" (Ephesians 2:8–9, HCSB).

What would happen if someone were to say, "I would rather do it myself. I don't have to rely on the gift (though it cost the Son of God's death). I choose to do it myself." The question is not hypothetical, for every day, people reject the Gospel and choose to "do it themselves." In the words of Dr. Phil, "How's that workin' out?"

Please don't miss this application in either of two ways. First, don't miss the giant cosmic application. If you have been trying to justify yourself, even the tiniest bit, stop it! Recognize that you cannot be good enough for God. Stop trying to make yourself pleasing and accept the reality that Christ presents us as a perfect offering to God. As a friend says, "If Jesus's death on the cross didn't make God happy (big theological word: *propitiation*), nothing you do is going to make Him happy.

Then don't miss the smaller but critically important application: you can't forgive you. That's God's job. His forgiveness is a gift. Accept it.

Now, having said that, we need to come back and say that accepting forgiveness for yourself and living with the reality that you are forgiven is absolutely essential. You don't need to be forgiven over and over for the same sin. You do, however, need to dip yourself again and again in the reality that if you are in Christ, you are a new creation.

Action Step Five: The *Freedom* of Forgiveness

Let me suggest you write Scripture on cards to read and memorize. Here are just some suggestions, but know that the Bible is absolutely full of affirmations of God's forgiveness. That's what the Gospel is all about.

"He has rescued us from the domain of darkness and transferred us into the kingdom of the Son He loves, in whom we have redemption, the forgiveness of sins." (Colossians 1:13–14, HCSB)

"In him we have redemption through his blood, the forgiveness of sins, in accordance with the riches of God's grace" (Ephesians 1:7, NIV).

"If we confess our sins, [God] is faithful and righteous to forgive us our sins and to cleanse us from all unrighteousness" (1 John 1:9, HCSB).

God is the One who saves us, forgives us, and redeems us. Forgiving ourselves does not achieve forgiveness from sin. According to both passages in Ephesians, we cannot do anything to earn forgiveness; rather it is a gift of God's grace. Only God can forgive our sins against Him, but we have to confess them. That is the only requirement, confession.

When we as Christ-followers say, "I know God can forgive me, but I can't forgive myself," we are elevating our ability to forgive and seeking to take upon ourselves what is God's ability. True healing and freedom only occur when we can accept the forgiveness God so graciously wants to give each of us. When one is not completely accepting of God's forgiveness, you're essentially buying the lies that Christ's sacrifice on the cross was not sufficient.

How sweet the reality that if we confess our sins, wounds, failures, and false beliefs to God, He'll forgive, renew, transform, restore, and redeem us.

Join me on my website at www.patlayton.net for additional resources.

Step Six: The Great Exchange

Tears welled up from the depths of my soul. I felt as if they'd never stop. A dark night of sobbing in my bathtub was a major turning point for me. After reading the book I mentioned earlier that I had "happened upon," the truth of what I had done to my child, my *life*, finally sunk into my heart, and the grief overwhelmed me. My own choices had taken so much from me! I grieved over my sin, the struggles in my life, my wounded heart, and, most of all, my precious baby.

After thirty-three years of carrying those burdens myself, I finally gave it all to God and *really* understood His work on Calvary. For the first time, I understood the sin that Jesus had personally carried to the cross for me. I understood the darkness of my heart at a level far beyond my personal needs. I understood that I could not save myself, that I needed a rescuer. Not until that night did I grasp the amazing depth of my Rescuer's love for me.

As I cried, I washed as though I could wash away all the dirt and pain of my life. In truth, I scrubbed at my body the way a rape victim tries to wash away the violent invasion of her body. As I bathed, I grasped the meaning of the cross at a deeper level and gratefully accepted the sacrifice of the cross. I understood that Jesus Christ willingly gave His life for mine—to set me free, to heal me, and to redeem my entire life.

Gradually, the tears for my own loss transformed into tears for the incredible burden that Jesus took on Himself and the passionate love that drove Him to shoulder it. My burden was more than I could bear, but He bore the burden of every person on the planet.

I began that night, releasing tears filled with my sins, my hurts, and my burdens. I finally and fully surrendered my heart.

The cleansing I felt was amazing! It was wonderful! It still is.

God wants that cleansing release for every one of His daughters.

In the last chapter, we made great progress in our journey toward forgiving those involved in the pain of our past. We also began to understand and accept God's forgiveness for us. The path of forgiveness is intertwined with the path of grieving. As our losses become more real to us, we will grieve more deeply, and in that grief, we'll need to revisit the step of forgiveness. As we move together to step six on our journey toward freedom, we'll focus on the importance of grieving our losses and receiving God's gift of wholeness.

Two Kinds of Sorrow

Any traumatic event in our lives will create sorrow. Many people experience deep sorrow that leads to depression, addictions, and a host of other dark places of the soul.

Grieving does not, however, have to be destructive. God

gave us the gift of grieving as a way to deal with life's difficulties and disappointments. The apostle Paul explained the difference between two kinds of sorrow in his second letter to the Corinthian church. He actually said he was glad the Corinthians were experiencing sorrow.

> Now I'm glad—not that you were upset, but that you were jarred into turning things around. You let the distress bring you to God, not drive you from him. The result was all gain, no loss. Distress that drives us to God ... turns us around. It gets us back in the way of salvation. We never regret that kind of pain. But those who let distress drive them away from God are full of regrets, and end up on a deathbed of regrets. And now, isn't it wonderful all the ways in which this distress has goaded you closer to God? You're more alive, more concerned, more sensitive, more reverent, more human, more passionate, more responsible. Looked at from this angle, you've come out of this with purity of heart.
>
> 2 Corinthians 7:9–11, The Message

Paul differentiates between godly distress/ sorrow and destructive distress/sorrow. Godly sorrow causes someone to turn back to God. It leads to repentance and never causes regret. On the other hand, destructive sorrow drives people away from God and does cause regret.

In past chapters, we discovered the importance of replacing lies—false beliefs we've embraced—with truth from God. If we'll allow our pain and sorrow to drive us toward God rather than away from Him, we'll experience transformation, healing, and new life.

Because past memories, sorrow, and hurts are uncomfortable for us, we try to avoid them or find ways to escape the pain. And yet, Paul was happy about the Corinthians' struggles and distress because it jarred them into change. Jesus also promoted godly sorrow and gave those who are hurting a wonderful promise: "Blessed are those who mourn, because they will be comforted" (Matthew 5:4, HCSB).

Jesus promises comfort to those who mourn. Remembering and grieving our losses are vital in the healing process. This allows us to remember where we have come from and how God worked in those circumstances.

Our Trustworthy Guide

As we're truly open about our feelings with God, He'll take us further down the path to healing. Most of us, though, have doubts about God's goodness and, specifically, about His heart toward us personally. Let's see what God says about us:

> "Do not be afraid, for I have ransomed you. I have called you by name; you are mine. When you go through deep waters, I will be with you. When you go through rivers of difficulty, you will not drown. When you walk through the fire of oppression, you will not be burned up; the flames will not consume you. For I am the Lord, your God, the Holy One of Israel, your Savior."
>
> Isaiah 43:1–3, NLT

"On that day you will not be put to shame for all the wrongs you have done to me, because I will remove from this city those who rejoice in their pride. Never again will you be haughty on my holy hill. But I will leave within you the meek and humble, who trust in the name of the Lord. . . . The Lord has taken away your punishment, he has turned back your enemy. The Lord, the King of Israel, is with you; never again will you fear any harm. . . . The Lord your God is with you, he is mighty to save. He will take great delight in you, he will quiet you with his love, he will rejoice over you with singing."

Zephaniah 3:11–12, 15, 17, NIV

God gave Isaiah several assurances when he faced various fears. He promised to be with Isaiah. Difficulties would not drown him, oppression would not burn him, nor would the flames of oppression consume him.

God promised that He won't put His children to shame (Zephaniah 3:11) and will take away our punishment (Zephaniah 3:15). However, God does require us to embrace some vital heart attitudes. He wants us to be meek, humble, and trusting.

Zephaniah 3:17 says that God takes delight in us and rejoices over us. Doesn't that provide you such comfort?

Fear is often the greatest enemy to meaningful life change. We long to return to what's familiar rather than take risks and face the unknown. More than anything else, the healing journey requires that we trust God. Healing the wounds in our innermost being will lead us down paths we never could have imagined. So we take one day and one step at a time as we walk into the shadows with Jesus. We allow Him to turn the shadows to light, to ease our pain, and to lead us into freedom, truth, and the desires of our hearts.

We have focused on the vital step of grieving our losses. The next step in our journey will open our minds and hearts to the incredible vistas that await us at the summit of our climb. We can become more than we've been and more than we realize. It's time to make the great exchange—to accept who we really are in Christ.

Change from the Inside Out

God's forgiveness, which comes with our confession, is a powerful force in our lives. God's blessings don't stop when we receive salvation. He wants to help us really change. That happens through our repentance. Unfortunately, that word has been given a bad connotation over the years.

Repent comes from the Greek word *metanoia*, which means to change (*meta*) our mind or understanding (*noia*). The word *metamorphosis* is a related term, meaning a change in form or substance, and is used to describe what occurs when a caterpillar retreats into its cocoon to emerge as a butterfly. This is a wondrous thing, but God does even more wondrous things for His children.

"Pay attention, O Jacob,
 for you are my servant, O Israel.
I, the Lord, made you,
 and I will not forget you.
I have swept away your sins like a cloud.
 I have scattered your offenses like the morning mist.
Oh, return to me,
 for I have paid the price to set you free."
Sing, O heavens, for the LORD has done this wondrous thing.
 Shout for joy, O depths of the earth!
Break into song,
 O mountains and forests and every tree!
For the Lord has redeemed Jacob
 and is glorified in Israel.

Isaiah 44:21–23, NLT

God's words in Isaiah 44 apply to the history of Israel, but they also give us an excellent starting place for our repentance. According to verses 21–22, God not only will not forget each one of us, but He also sweeps away our sins. He scatters them like the mist and has paid the price of our freedom.

Romans 12:1–2 and John 8:31–32 clarify further by separating the process of repentance or transformation into God's part and our part.

I urge you, brothers, in view of God's mercy, to offer your bodies as living sacrifices, holy and pleasing to God—this is your spiritual act of worship. Do not conform any longer to the pattern of this world, but be transformed by the renewing of your mind. Then you will be able to test and approve what God's will is—His good, pleasing, and perfect will.

Romans 12:1–2, NIV

Jesus said ... "If you continue in My word, you really are My disciples. You will know the truth, and the truth will set you free."

John 8:31–32, HCSB

God doesn't expect you to change your own life. He asks that you make yourself available to His Holy Spirit by remaining in His presence. As we turn to God and begin to give Him our secrets, our shame, false beliefs, and distorted perspectives, we become engaged in a battle of the mind and heart. Recall the model we discussed in step 2 in which our wounds become infected with lies that lead to destructive agreements and a false sense of self.

For though we live in the world, we do not wage war as the world does. The weapons we fight with are not the weapons of the world. On the contrary, they have divine power to demolish strongholds. We demolish arguments and every pretension that sets itself up against the knowledge of God, and we take captive every thought to make it obedient to Christ.

2 Corinthians 10:3–5, NIV

The cosmic battle between good and evil is not waged on earth. It occurs in a realm that we cannot see or even really understand. We must demolish the "strongholds" that set themselves up against God. Today we don't use the word *stronghold* very often. Imagine castles, fortresses, or even a battle scene from a movie like *Braveheart* or *Lord of the Rings*. Strongholds are enemy fortresses in our territory made of lies that we have allowed to take root in our lives. Anything that is contrary to God and His Word can become an enemy foothold.

Destroying these fortresses of falsehood takes a lot of time, muscle, and energies. In my life, I imagine massive armies attacking and weapons such as cannons and explosives crumbling these structures to the ground.

As we recognize the battle being waged over our minds and hearts, we begin to understand why change must occur from the inside out. God must do the work in our innermost being — our hearts and minds. He transforms us. Our part in repentance is to persistently decide to turn or return to God.

Grieving Our Losses

God sees your pain, your losses, and shame. He not only gives you permission to grieve your losses, but He invites you to grieve. Grief is the process God created to help us deal with the inevitable losses of life. As you come to grips with the sorrow of your heartbreak, then you can leave it at Jesus's feet—where grace and mercy meet. God longs to comfort you and to set you free, so you can lift your head.

While it may be painful, it is important to acknowledge the "crummy stuff"—those things, opportunities, people, relationships, experiences, or feelings that have been altered by your struggles. If you are one who journals or has been keeping a journal during the time you have been reading this book, I want to encourage you to write about the things God brings to your mind.

Now close your eyes and imagine Jesus walking into the room, putting His arms around you, and gently speaking these words to you:

"Do not be afraid, for I have ransomed you. I have called you by name; you are mine. When you go through deep waters, I will be with you. When you go through rivers of difficulty, you will not drown. When you walk through the fire of oppression, you will not be burned up; the flames will not consume you. For I am the Lord, your God, the Holy One of Israel, your Savior."

Isaiah 43:1–3, NLT

All Things New

Too often we see ourselves as the sum of all our failures. We get blinded to who we really are and how God sees us after we've placed our trust in Jesus to rescue and redeem us. According to 2 Corinthians 5:17–18, if anyone is in Christ, he or she becomes a "new creation." This passage means that when you come to accept Christ as your Lord and Savior you become new. Your old desires, your old inclinations, and your old nature have been replaced with godly desires and a nature that He has given you. According to the verses from Ezekiel, God has given us His Spirit, which causes us to want to follow His ways.

> Therefore, if anyone is in Christ, he is a new creation; the old has gone, the new has come! All this is from God, who reconciled us to himself through Christ and gave us the ministry of reconciliation.
>
> 2 Corinthians 5:17–18, NIV

The Old Testament prophet Ezekiel provided us a beautiful picture of the new life Christ provides for us.

> "I will sprinkle clean water on you, and you will be clean; I will cleanse you from all your filthiness and from all your idols. Moreover, I will give you a new heart and put a new spirit within you; and will remove the heart of stone from your flesh and give you a heart of flesh. I will put my Spirit

within you and cause you to walk in My statutes, and you will be careful to follow My ordinances . . . you will be My people, and I will be your God."

Ezekiel 36:25–28, NASB

Amazingly, God makes us entirely new creations when we place our faith in Jesus. For several reasons, most of us never experience much of the new creation God intends for us because:

- The enemy continues to deceive us, telling us God doesn't care and that we're nothing.
- We continue to live out of the well-worn patterns and ruts in our lives and don't embrace our new hearts and new lives.
- We block the work of the Holy Spirit by resisting Him or turning away from God, going our own way, and seeking satisfaction apart from Him.

God has so much more for you and me. He has placed us in a favored position in His family, and we can step up to occupy that status as favored daughters.

Your Favored Position in God's Family

God's love is lavished on those who place their faith in Jesus. Because of nothing other than God's extreme love for us, we've been given a position that few of us have grasped, and even fewer live in. Our enemy clearly wants to keep this hidden, but Scripture clearly tells us we "did not receive a spirit of slavery to fall back into fear, but you received the Spirit of adoption, by whom we cry out, 'Abba, Father!' The Spirit Himself testifies together with our spirit that we are God's children" (Romans 8:15–16, HCSB).

When we become children of God, we receive some amazing privileges. We are God's sons or daughters. We have literally been adopted into His family, but we also become heirs, which means we have an inheritance.

We've already been granted the privilege of the firstborn, but our position as royalty won't be fully revealed until Jesus returns in His glory. "When Christ, who is our life, is revealed, then you also will be revealed with Him in glory" (Colossians 3:4, NASB). We participate spiritually in His death, resurrection, and glorification. We're daughters of the King of kings, coheirs with Christ!

God wants this favored status to affect the way we approach life, the enemy, and enslavement to past sins and failures. Romans 8:15 plainly says that we have received a spirit of adoption and not of slavery or fear. That should give us some boldness, sisters!

Trading Sorrows for Joy

The Bible is full of prophecies and promises that God will fulfill, in part now, and to the fullest extent when Jesus comes to take us into His eternal kingdom. Jeremiah 31 gives us one of these exciting prophecies for Israel, which also applies to Christ-followers under the new covenant. Look at the passage and think how it fits both now and later.

> "They will come home and sing songs of joy on the heights of Jerusalem. They will be radiant because of the LORD's good gifts—the abundant crops of grain, new wine, and olive oil, and the healthy flocks and herds. Their life will be like a watered garden, and all their sorrows will be gone. The young women will dance for joy, and the men—old and young—will join in the celebration. I will turn their mourning into joy. I will comfort them and exchange their sorrow for rejoicing. The priests will enjoy abundance, and my people will feast on my good gifts. I, the LORD, have spoken!"
>
> Jeremiah 13:12–14, NLT

Although our current lives will still have troubles, God has given us His comfort, which should cause us to rejoice greatly. Read verse 13 again: God will turn our mourning into joy and our sorrow into rejoicing. Yes, even our sorrow. Trust me, but more importantly, trust Him.

Action Step Six: Today is Your Day!

At this point in your journey, it's important for you to completely receive the gift of your salvation! It is time of you to fully embrace what happened with Jesus at the cross for *you*! True and lasting freedom only comes as we understand the ransom price Jesus paid for our freedom and as we accept His payment as our only hope of salvation and real life.

Steps to the Cross

1. God created you and loves you. (Genesis 1:26–27; John 3:16–18)

2. We've fallen from our original glory. (Genesis 3:1, 13; Romans 3:23)

3. Jesus came to rescue you from darkness and captivity. (Colossians 1:12–14)

4. Jesus is your only hope for abundant and eternal life. (John 14:6)

5. You must choose life. (John 1:12–13; John 5:24)

Using these five points, if you have never done it before or if you just want to mark today as *the day*, speak or write out a simple prayer to surrender your life to Christ today.

If you have questions about accepting Jesus's sacrifice and

free gift of eternal salvation, please ask your pastor, Christian friend, or another committed Christian you know. I want to hear from you. Email me at patlayton@mac.com and I will send you a *free gift* from me to you!

Next—tell someone else! A friend, family member, that person you know has been praying for you!

Then—tell the world! ☺

Join me on my website at www.patlayton.net for additional resources.

Step Seven: The Peace of Release

I have always been an avid reader and writer. I've kept a prayer journal for more than thirty years, chronicling my healing journey and pouring out my emotions. Under my bed, I keep a stash of yellowing, spiral-bound notebooks. They share my story—one of a broken woman rescued by a mighty God. They're so personal—full of testimonies to God's grace, but also selfishness and silliness and whining—that I don't know what I want done with them when I go home to Him.

With the beginnings of those notebooks, I took my first look into God's Word. Apart from the ambiguities of the world, God's Word answered my questions clearly. I remember when God showed me Psalm 139:13–16 (NLT):

> You made all the delicate, inner parts of my body and knit me together in my mother's womb. Thank you for making me so wonderfully complex! Your workmanship is marvelous—how well I know it. You watched me as I was being formed in utter seclusion, as I was woven together in the dark of the womb. *You saw me before I was born. Every day of my life was recorded in your book. Every moment was laid out before a single day had passed.* (NLT, emphasis mine)

As I envisioned my aborted child, my heart dropped. My grief encompassed me. As I learned how God felt about my baby— about every baby— I experienced fresh pain. I cried. I collapsed to the bedroom floor and buried my head in my arms. I cried out, this time to God, in sorrow and in the solitude of my significant loss. Tears welled up from the depths of my soul, and it felt as if they'd never stop.

It was then the Lord gave me a vision, of a little girl in a frilly pink dress. She was beautiful with long blonde hair and short arms outstretched to me. She smiled and then said, "It's okay, Mommy. I am happy here with Jesus. I forgive you and love you. I'll be here waiting when you come, but Jesus has some things for you to do first."

This is the final step toward finding Peace with Your Past!

To seal the deal, so to speak, will you allow God to shine the light of His love into the heartache of your past heartbreak?

Just look at where you have come already. How precious and great is our God! Since you said *yes* you have:

1.   Boldly stepped beyond fear and came forward to trust God with your secret pain. You have had the courage to share your story.
2.   Looked at some buried truth about the ways the enemy attempts to keep you in captivity and faced some difficult facts about the sinful nature of women and men.
3.   Dealt with masks of anger.
4.   Embraced unforgiveness to set yourself and others free.
5.   And best of *all,* looked into the face of your Lord to understand your own sin and receive His marvelous, unmatched mercy, grace, and forgiveness.

What Jesus Has Done with Your Past Failures and Sins

Surely our grief He Himself bore, and our sorrows He carried; yet we ourselves esteemed Him stricken, smitten of God, and afflicted. But He was pierced through for our transgressions, He was crushed for our iniquities; the chastening for our well being fell upon Him, and by His scourging we are healed.

Isaiah 53:4–5, NASB

Let all that I am praise the LORD;
  may I never forget the good things he does for me.
He forgives all my sins
  and heals all my diseases.
He redeems me from death
  and crowns me with love and tender mercies. . . .
For his unfailing love toward those who fear him
  is as great as the height of the heavens above the earth.
He has removed our sins as far from us
  as the east is from the west.
The LORD is like a father to his children,
  tender and compassionate to those who fear him.

Psalm 103:2–4, 11–13, NLT

Action Step Seven: Celebrate!

It is time for a ceremony or a celebration that will allow you to *"mark"* this day as one of closure and release. From this point forward, you are going to allow God to make your story different. To create a *new ending* for the pain of your past.

Find a way to celebrate that best suits who God created you to be.

- Write a letter.
- Host a sweet praise party with some close friends.
- Go on a celebration cruise!
- Release some balloons as you declare the release of your past to the capable hand of your heavenly Father.

This is *huge*!!

I am picturing a friend releasing many long and terrifying years of childhood sexual abuse at the hands of her mother's lover; another who lost her beloved mother at eight years old and ended up in the hands of a nasty stepmother not much different from Cinderella; another whose husband was less than creative and chose her best friend over her; another whose traumatic loss of a baby boy while in the care of a beloved family member has kept her in unforgiveness and bondage most of her adult life.

I am picturing you, my friend. Although we have not met, like you, I have experienced that life-changing freedom of finding peace with my past. Trust me here, God wants to engage that newfound freedom of yours as He seeks out the lost and lonely of the world to discover His redeeming love!

Use the space below to list some ways you will celebrate the journey of freedom God has led you through.

Join me on my website at **www.patlayton.net** for additional resources.

Step Eight: Moving from Your Past to Your Purpose

We have traveled an amazing journey together. We are not the same women who picked up this book and wondered if we could *ever* be completely free, if we could ever truly get past the pain of the past. We wondered what in the world God might be doing with the mess that life seems to be *now*—in our present. God has been good. He has begun a powerful work of healing in us, and He has brought us to a new time and place. Even though the path ahead is unfamiliar, we're ready to move forward into all He has in store for us.

Your Ongoing Journey

As we close this workbook, please realize that completing the eight steps to *Getting Past Your Past* doesn't mean your journey is completed. It's actually just beginning.

I used the quote in my book *Life Unstuck* that says, "When we turn to God with the pain of our past, we are met by a God who has plans for our future!"

That entire book was based upon the stunning words found in Psalm 139 but really solidified by verse 16, which says: "All the days ordained for me were written in your book before one of the came to be (NIV).

You've kept track of my every toss and turn through the sleepless nights, each tear entered in your ledger, each ache written in our book. . . I'm proud to praise God, proud to praise God. Fearless now, I trust in God: what can mere mortals do to me? God, you did everything you promised, and I'm thanking you with all my heart. You pulled me from the brink of death, my felt from the cliff edge of doom. Now I stroll at leisure with God in the sunlit fields of life.

Psalm 56:8, 10–13, The Message

God is calling you into a great adventure. He has a unique role just for you. As you step outside yourself to engage in the larger story, acknowledge that completing the first pass through the eight steps to healing doesn't mean there's nothing else for you.

Here's some of what God has in store for you as you continue the journey with Him:

I pray that out of His glorious riches he may strengthen you with power through his Spirit and your inner being, so that Christ may dwell in your hearts through faith. And I pray that you, being rooted and established in love, may have power, together with all the saints, to grasp how wide and long and high and deep is the love of Christ, and to know this love that surpasses knowledge— that you may be filled to the measure of all the fullness of God. Now to him who is able to do immeasurable more than all we ask or imagine, according to his power that is a work within us, to him be glory in the church and in Christ Jesus throughout all generations, forever and ever! Amen.

Ephesians 3:16–21, NIV

We speak of God's secret wisdom, a wisdom that has been hidden and that God destined for our glory before time began. . . as it is written: "No eye has seen, nor ear has heard, nor mind has conceived what God has prepared for those who love him."

1 Corinthians 2:7-9, ERV

The Power of Your Story

God's provisions for the past are not only sufficient, but His promises for our future are incredibly bright! God invites us to become instruments of His love, His life, and His healing power. God has led us on a path of wellness. Now He wants to use our stories to help others. Our next objective must be to discover and pursue God's purposes for our lives.

Revelation 12:11 unfolds the larger story and the coming final battle between good and evil: "They overcome him by the blood of the Lamb [Jesus], and by the word of their testimony they did not love their lives so much as to shrink away for earth (NIV).

In Revelation 12:11, "they" refers to us—Jesus's followers. "Him" who will be overcome refers to the enemy. What three things are crucial in overcoming the work of the enemy? How can our stories or testimonies be powerful in the battle?

Live Your Story

Remember these three key truths as you pursue your role in the larger story:

Key1: God wants us to live for something greater than ourselves.

> For everything, absolutely everything, above and below, visible and invisible, rank after rank after rank of angels –everything got started in him and finds its purpose in him. Colossians 1–16, The Message

> I chose you before I formed you in the womb; I set you apart before you were born. I appointed you a prophet to the nations.
>
> Jeremiah 1:5, HCSB

Key 2: We are saved to serve God. We are healed to serve others.

> Don't be ashamed of the testimony about our Lord, or of me His prisoner. Instead, share in suffering for the gospel, relying on the power of God.
>> He has saved us and called us
>> with a holy calling,
>> not according to our works,
>> but according to His own purpose and
> grace,
>> which was given to us in Christ Jesus
>> before time began.
>>
>> 2 Timothy 1:8–9, HCSB

Do you not know that your body is a sanctuary for the Holy Spirit who is in you, whom you have from God? You are not your own, for were bought at a price; therefore, glorify God in your body.

1 Corinthians 6:19–20, HCSB

Key 3: God's power is revealed in our weakness.

Brothers, consider your calling: Not many are wise from a human perspective, not many powerful, not many of noble birth. Instead, God has chosen the world's foolish things to shame the wise, and God has chosen the world's weak things to shame the strong. God has chosen the world's insignificant and despised things, the things viewed as nothing, so He might bring to nothing the things that are viewed as something, so that no one can boast in His presence. But from Him you are in Christ Jesus, who for us became wisdom from God as well as righteousness, sanctification, and redemption.

2 Corinthians 1:26-30, HCSB

Setting Hearts Free

The amazing thing is that as you work with Jesus in setting captives free, you'll find that one of the captives that's becoming more increasingly liberated is you! God has made some amazing promises to us if we are willing to raise our eyes to Him (above our current pain) and embrace the larger story. These promises give powerful incentive not to give up, but to continue on to still more.

Thousands of women, bound by secrets; wear masks for fear of not being accepted and are sitting in our churches, living as our neighbors, and they may even be our closest friends. Your sharing could help set them free.

Using wisdom and prayer to guide your sharing is very important. God will show you how, when, where, and with whom. God would not have you injure or hurt others in the process of sharing your story.

Think back to the first time you opened this book. A common thread shared with thousands of women is the fear of being *real* in front of one another. Sometimes those painful experiences connect us. Thousands more could identify with you as a result of your being real and sharing the losses of your past, the struggle of your present, and the dreams of your future.

Women need one another.

I need you and I am grateful to have touched a tiny place in your life as you have allowed God to take you on this journey of finding peace with your past. Now, go and live it, sister!

Pat

Action Step Eight: How Can I Share What God Has Done for Me?!

As we learn to accept and appreciate who we really are in Him and who He really is in us, God has an adventure waiting for us.

As you join with Jesus in His mission to bind up the brokenhearted, set captives free, and replace beauty for ashes, you won't believe how exciting and deeply fulfilling that can be!

- Discuss with your prayer partner(s) what cautions you might need to exercise as you begin to share your story with others.

- With whom might you speak to privately before sharing your story publicly? Your husband? Parents? Children?

- Brainstorm ways you may use your healing story to reach out to other women who are hurting and still in bondage.

- Establish some sort of accountability with one another about how you will serve God in helping others as you have been helped. Only the truth, which you now have, can help set them free.

- How willing are you to participate in the adventure of setting hearts free? What, if any, reservations do you have?

- What unique gifts, talents, resources, and life experiences has God given you to comfort hurting people, to release them from bondage, or to show them the way to Jesus so they may find redemption from shame and failures?

- How might people respond to your encouragement that there is a way out of their problems, pain, and destructive behaviors?

Continually review this material, especially your personal notes, to remind yourself of God's promise to you.

Keep God's Word in your mouth and in your heart. Remember, we have decided to embrace life!

Although you've completed *Healing a Woman's Heart*, the rest of your life is a continuing journey with Christ. In life, there will always be mountains to climb until we reach our heavenly destination. So, as you go forward, be good to yourself, take time to love yourself, protect your freedom, and keep your sense of humor.

Your *Daily* Affirmation!

Read Isaiah 61:1–3 aloud, replacing "me" with your name.

> The Spirit of the Sovereign Lord is on me, because the Lord has anointed me to preach good news to the poor. He has sent me to bind up the brokenhearted, to proclaim freedom for the captives and release from darkness for the prisoners, to proclaim the year of the Lord's favor and the day of vengeance of our God, to comfort all who mourn and provide for those who grieve in Zion-to bestow on them a crown of beauty instead of ashes, the oil of gladness instead of mourning, and a garment of praise instead of a spirit of despair.
>
> Isaiah 61:1–3, NIV

Speak the following affirmation, based on God's Word, daily:

> I am woman of truth and my identity is in Christ and I am who He says I am. I am a new creation in Christ. The fears and losses of the past that appeared to be a mountain from below are now under my feet. God has been faithful to do what He said He would do for me. I am His and He is mine. He has set me free.

For Extra Study

Bless be the God and Father of our Lord Jesus
Christ, the Father of mercies and the God of all
comfort. He comforts us in all our affliction, so
that we may be able to comfort those who are in
any kind of affliction; through the comfort we
ourselves receive from God. For as the sufferings
of Christ overflow to us, so our comfort overflows
through Christ.

2 Corinthians 1:3–-5, HCSB

But thanks be to God, who always leads us in
triumph in Christ, and manifests through us the
sweet aroma of the knowledge of Him in every
place. For we are a fragrance of Christ to God
among those who are being saved and among
those who are perishing to the one aroma from
death to death, to the other an aroma from life to
life. And who is adequate for these things?

2 Corinthians 2 14–-16, HCSB

So teach us to number our days,
That we may gain a heart of wisdom.

Psalm 90:12, (NKJV)

But as for you, you meant evil against me; but God meant it for good, in order to bring it about as it is this day, to save many people alive.

Genesis 50:20, NKJV

And you shall know the truth, and the truth shall make you free."

John 8:32, NKJV

Thank you for joining this eight-step journey of getting past your past and on with your purpose. Please follow my website for group and online coaching.

Please join Pat as she strives to inspire women in the QUEST of faith! www.patlayton.net

ABOUT THE AUTHOR

Pat is a busy speaker, writer, and life coach. She is the published author of six books. After founding and leading a multifaceted ministry for women in Tampa, Florida, her international abortion recovery Bible study *Surrendering the Secret* was published by Lifeway in 2008. The study has reached thousands of women and men and since been translated into Spanish and Chinese. She has appeared on several major TV and radio networks including Focus on the Family and Life Today. Pat's book, *Life UnStuck:* Peace with the Past, Purpose in the Present, and Passion for the Future, released in spring 2015. She is a wife of over forty years, mom of three, mother-in-love of two lovely women, and "G" (grandmother) of five. She and her husband, Mike live on a "Hobby Farm" with lots of critters in NW Georgia. Every spare moment that is not filled with "all of the above" is stolen for rocking on her front porch, drinking sweet tea and reading inspirational fiction or a decorating magazine.

Pat's determined purpose is to experience God more passionately each and every day of her life, and for that passion to make a Kingdom difference in the lives of others.

You can join her in the quest of faith at www.patlayton.net where she shares everything but the sweet tea!

You May Also Like:

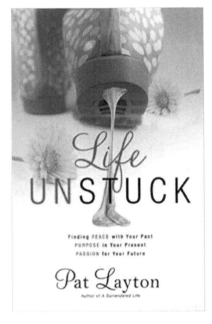

Everyone has felt *stuck* at some point in life. Our inertia is gone, momentum is wiped out, and life trudges on devoid of passion. But God has so much more than this planned for his daughters. With passion and enthusiasm, Pat Layton invites women to imagine their world *unstuck*--a place where they feel at peace with the past, find purpose in the present, and revel in the possibilities that the future holds. With her rousing Unstuck Manifesto, she delves deep into the areas readers get stuck in the most--relationships, finances, ministry, career, and more--and, with the Scriptures as her guide, unveils the path to positive forward movement.

Available on Amazon and Barnes & Noble!

Surrendering the Secret: Healing the Heartbreak of Abortion - Learner Guide provides a personal study experience helping hurting women find the path to healing through honest, interactive Bible study; meaningful group experiences; unique journaling exercises; and confidential, caring community.

Many women hide the secret of abortion deep in their hearts and they are suffering severe consequences. They carry a great burden of shame and failure, afraid to reveal their hidden pain, and by doing so are forced to endure the long-lasting effects in isolation. Surrendering the Secret will allow women to release this burden and find freedom through 'redemptive community' while experiencing hope and joy, as shame and failure are replaced with beauty.

Available on Amazon and Lifeway!

JOIN THE NEW

Unstuck Woman Club

We have MOVED from
Facebook to Face to Face!

FREE MONTHLY GIFTS AND GATHERINGS

To Register Visit
patlayton.podia.com

VISIT

PATLAYT N.NET

FOR FREE RESOURCES, EVENTS

AND

ONLINE COURSES

Made in the USA
Columbia, SC
24 February 2021